Beading

A beginner's step-by-step guide to beading techniques

DIANA VOWLES

Design Originals

an Imprint of Fox Chapel Publishing
www.d-originals.com

Diana Vowles is a writer, artist and craftsperson whose bead jewelry has featured at major fashion shows and society events. She draws inspiration for her designs from elements as varied as antique jacquard textiles and lace to the natural world. She translates these ideas into beautiful and intricate pieces of wearable art, using beads from her large collection assembled from sources worldwide.

Copyright © 2012 Arcturus Publishing Limited

First published in the United Kingdom by Arcturus Publishing Limited, 2012.
First published in North America in 2013, revised, by Design Originals, an imprint of Fox Chapel Publishing, 1970 Broad Street, East Petersburg, PA 17520.

ISBN 978-1-57421-503-8

Cover images: Shutterstock

Printed in China
First printing

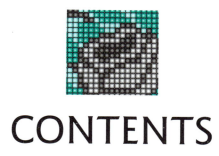

CONTENTS

INTRODUCTION

Since the earliest days of humankind and in all societies, the urge to make art and to decorate one's body has been a constant theme – and drilling holes in shells, bones and pieces of wood so that they could be threaded on a cord was a way of making jewelry that required no technology and few resources. From those primitive beginnings eventually came the vast array of beads and styles of using them that we have today.

Making bead jewelry is endlessly satisfying and can be done by anyone blessed with a little patience and the ability to find pleasure in crafting beautiful objects with their hands. In our modern world, where so much depends on digital technology, it is a joy in itself to sit down with some beads, some thread and a few simple tools, and fashion something pretty to adorn someone's neck or wrist.

Bead jewelry is also endlessly versatile; using precious metals and semiprecious gemstones, you can make pieces that could be worn at the most elegant evening parties; with a leather thong and a few chunky beads, you can create folk-art-style necklaces and bracelets in little more than minutes; or you can draw elaborate designs for woven bead chokers with the pattern continuing into long fringing that will lie against the wearer's throat and chest, and spend days threading them. This is a form of jewelry-making that is suited to all tastes and by experimentation you'll find out which type of beading you love the best.

Whether you plan to work with beads just for pleasure or have an eye to making jewelry to sell, this book will provide you with a grounding in how to make a successful start. While the equipment needed isn't complicated, it's always best to get the right tool for the job to avoid frustrating delays and perhaps damage to your beads – so don't feel that for the time being you can get by with some DIY-store pliers from the toolbox as this may discourage you from trying to progress further.

Buying the beads, of course, is much more fun. Beading is now a popular craft and there are many well-stocked bead stores to be found – and with the benefit of the internet, you can buy beads worldwide. You'll be able to revel in the colors, patterns and materials that are presented before your eyes and just seeing them will prompt all kinds of design ideas in your head. Here the difficulty lies in restraining yourself from buying so many beads that it would take you years to use them all!

In this book you'll find three simple projects that will employ the skills you have learned in the previous pages. Once you have made these, you'll be itching to get on with your own projects, using your own designs and pushing your skills further. You may realize you have discovered a new career, or you may simply have developed an addiction to beading for pleasure! Whichever is the case, the journey will be a fascinating one.

PART ONE:
EQUIPMENT AND MATERIALS

THREADS

One of the first decisions you'll make about any piece of bead jewelry is the type of material you'll be threading your beads onto. There is a wide variety of threads available and your choice will largely rest on the style of beads and the techniques you will be using, as well as the look you want to achieve: sophisticated, folk art, softly draping or starkly geometric, for example. The following are the most popular materials to use, but keep a creative eye out for other choices; you'll soon develop an instinct for spotting more unusual materials that will work with the beads you want to use.

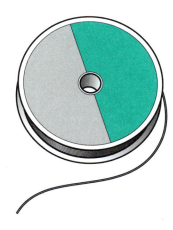

FLEXIBLE BEADING WIRE
This is made from fine strands of stainless steel twisted together and encased in plastic, so it is extremely strong. You can buy it in a variety of colors, thicknesses and strengths; the number of strands of steel also varies and the higher the number the more flexible the wire is. Some types can be knotted, but you will usually need to use crimps instead (p. 9). Take care to cover the cut ends to avoid scratches from the wire when the jewelry is worn.

POLYESTER AND SILK THREAD
Polyester thread is easily available from craft stores in a range of colors and thicknesses, including a fine one suitable for beadweaving. You will generally need to use a needle for threading, though it's possible to give a rigid end to the thicker threads by waxing them. Silk and embroidery threads have attractive finishes and a greater range of colors, but lack the strength of the synthetic threads.

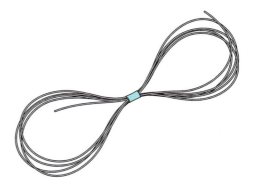

CORD

You can buy cord made of leather, satin, cotton, and hemp. Leather is popular with beaders as it doesn't fray and threads easily; it's also inexpensive and you'll be able to find it in a range of colors. It's well suited to rustic designs and chunky, handcrafted beads. Most fabric cord does fray, but painting the end with clear nail polish before you begin threading will solve the problem. Knotted cord can be as attractive in a necklace or bracelet as the beads themselves, so choose colors that will complement the overall color scheme to make the most of it.

BEADING ELASTIC

As beading elastic doesn't require a clasp, it is ideal threading material for a bracelet or necklace for a child or indeed any adult who may find opening and closing a small clasp difficult. It is available clear, or in various colors and in different thicknesses. The thicker cord is also stronger and easier to thread, so choose the thickest that will go comfortably through the beads you are using.

METAL WIRE

Not to be confused with beading wire, metal wire is available from bead and craft stores as well as bullion suppliers. You have a wide choice of material – brass, bronze, copper, silver, gold, and silver- and gold-plated – and also colors, though the color-coated wires may show signs of wear in time, as may the plated ones. While you're still developing your expertise, wastage may occur so, the cheaper metals such as copper, brass and plated wires are a good choice; sterling silver and gold are much more expensive.

Wire is sold in different thicknesses and in three grades of hardness: soft, half-hard and hard. Soft is suitable for wrapping round other wires, but lacks the strength needed for clasps; hard is, as you might expect, the opposite, and would be tricky to wrap successfully. Half-hard is a good multi-purpose choice. Always wear some form of eye protection when you are cutting wire.

MEMORY WIRE

Made from toughened steel and plated with silver or gold, memory wire retains its coiled shape. You can buy it on a reel or in ready-cut lengths for necklaces, bracelets and rings. It is very strong, making it ideal for heavy beads or those with roughened holes that might damage other threading materials, and requires special wire cutters.

FINDINGS

The term "findings" is used for the small items you will need for assembling most of your jewelry – clasps, bars, rings, pins and so on. There is a huge variety of findings available, in both plated and pure metals; sterling silver or gold are best for earwires and clasps that will rest on the skin, as some people are allergic to other forms of metal.

JUMP RINGS AND SPLIT RINGS
Small and simple, jump rings are probably the findings you will use the most. Just a metal ring with a split in it, a jump ring can be employed to link lengths of threading material or chain together, or to attach fastenings of all kinds. Split rings are similar but coiled like a key ring, making them more secure; this means they can be used as a ring to hook a clasp into.

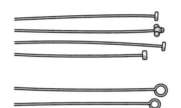

HEADPINS AND EYEPINS
These are used for making dangles of beads, such as for a drop earring. Headpins have a plain or decorative "stop" at the end that prevents your beads from falling off, while eyepins terminate in a loop from which you can attach further ornamentation.

EARRING FINDINGS

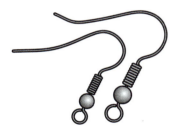

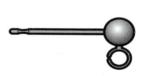

Fish hooks, the most popular choice for pierced ears, can be found in a range of sizes and styles, from just a simple curve of metal with a loop to take the earring decoration to more embellished designs.

Posts are ideal for discreet, simple earrings. They have a loop from which you can attach as many or as few beads as you wish.

Clip-on earring findings are for use on ears that are not pierced. A variation on the hinged type is the screw-on, which can be adjusted for the wearer's comfort.

Chandeliers are for those who like large, "statement" earrings. An elaborate version of a simple hoop and in a range of designs with a variable number of loops from which to attach a dangle of beads, they allow you to be as creative as you like.

CLASPS

S-hook clasps are easy to attach, making them useful for necklaces. If you want to make the length of the necklace adjustable you can finish the other end with a length of chain so that the clasp can be hooked into different links. However, as S-hook clasps are not fully closed they are less suitable for bracelets as they may come undone.

Bolt rings are secure but quite fiddly to use, especially as they are usually small. They are not a good choice for someone with arthritic fingers or limited mobility in their arms.

Parrot, trigger or lobster claw clasps are generally easier to use than bolt rings as they are more solid. They come in a range of metals, finishes and designs.

Magnetic clasps are the easiest of all to attach, but are better suited to necklaces than bracelets as they may also attach themselves to metal objects as the wearer goes out and about. Note that magnetic clasps should never be worn by anyone with a pacemaker.

Slider clasps, also known as tube bar clasps, are available in different lengths and with a variable number of loops, making them versatile for multistrand necklaces and bracelets. One side of the fastening simply slots into the other and locks into place.

Box clasps tend to be traditional in appearance and are available for single or multistrand pieces. One side of the clasp is a tongue that slides into the decorative side and locks into place, making it a secure fastening.

Barrel, or screw, clasps are very secure but require two hands to tighten them properly, so are unsuitable for bracelets.

Toggles are very easy to use and the range of colors, materials and designs is very large. To attach the clasp the toggle is pulled through the ring, so if you are using large beads you will need to add a few at the end of your necklace or bracelet that are smaller than the ring.

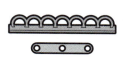
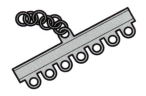

SPACER BARS AND END BARS
For use with multistrand necklaces or bracelets, these may be quite plain or more ornamental. Spacer bars are, as you might expect, a way of keeping the strands spaced apart; end bars have a fastening or just a loop to which a fastening can be attached.

END CONES
These come in a range of designs and are an attractive way to finish multistrand pieces.

CRIMPS
To finish the ends of wire or thread you will need to use crimps, which are slipped on and tightened with pliers.

LEATHER CRIMPS AND SPRING ENDS
These are used to finish the ends of leather and fabric cord, with a loop to which you can attach a fastener.

CALOTTES
Calottes are a form of crimp, concealing the end of your thread but with a loop too for the fastening to attach to. They are hinged at the side or the bottom.

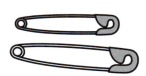

SAFETY PINS
An easy way of making informal, contemporary jewelry, safety pins are easily available but can be bought in bead stores in a range of colors for decorative effect.

EXTENSION CHAIN
For making bracelets or necklaces that may need to be adjusted to the wearer's size, an extension chain gives plenty of choice as to the exact length.

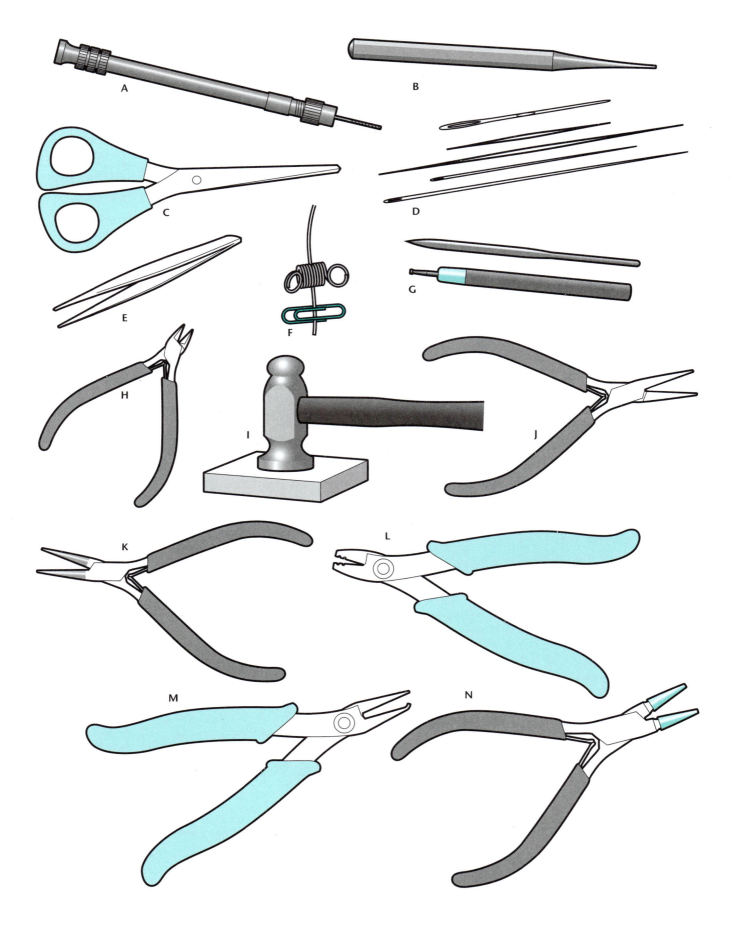

TOOLS

Some of the tools needed for making bead jewelry can be found in DIY stores, while for others you will need to visit bead stores, either in person or online. It's worth getting exactly the right equipment, as a few dollars saved in purchases can add up to hours of unnecessary fiddling and perhaps damaged beads or fastenings too.

A Reamer
This is an important piece of equipment, especially if you will be using seed beads for weaving. This handy tool comes with a variety of diamond-tipped files for smoothing and enlarging the holes in your beads where necessary. Always keep the files and beads wet while using, partly to prevent damage to the bead and reamer but also to avoid breathing in harmful dust.

B Awl
You will need to move knots along your threads to get them placed exactly right, and using an awl is the best way to do it. Another implement such as a large needle or cocktail stick can be used as a substitute, but the large handle of the awl makes the job easier.

C Scissors
Ordinary household scissors will suffice, as long as they are sharp. For close work, a small pair with sharply pointed blades will be easiest to maneuver.

D Needles
For some tasks, such as stringing large beads, strong, blunt-ended needles that can be bought in an accessory department will suffice, but for beadweaving you will need to buy long, extra-fine needles from a bead store. There you will also find needles that have a long eye running down the center, which are much easier to thread.

E Tweezers
Fine-pointed tweezers are invaluable for untangling knots and picking up small beads. The ones sold in bead stores are best suited for the job.

F Bead stopper
You will want to make sure that when you are working with beads they are not going to fall off the end of your thread. A bead stopper is a handy little device, although in the absence of one a paperclip will do.

G Files
The end of a length of metal wire will need to be smoothed to avoid it scratching the wearer. An emery board will suffice, but as always the proper tool will save time and a metal file from a bead store is preferable. A wire rounder, which has a cup burr at the tip, is ideal for rounding the end of a wire; just insert the wire into the cup and turn the wire rounder back and forth. Don't use it for memory wire, though, as this will destroy the inside of the cup.

H Wire cutters
So that you can get in close to your work, buy wire cutters with small, pointed ends. Memory wire is so strong it will ruin ordinary wire cutters; use cutters intended for the purpose, or heavy-duty cutters from a DIY store.

I Hammer and block
Hammering wire gives it interesting texture and shape. The best hammer to buy is one that is flat at one end and rounded at the other, and you will also need a steel block to lay the wire on.

J Flat-nose pliers
These pliers have flat jaws and are used for myriad purposes, such as attaching findings and fastenings and making angles in wire.

K Round-nose pliers
As the name suggests, round-nose pliers have rounded jaws that taper to a point. Use them for making wire loops; if you wish to make a series of loops of the same size, mark the jaws to help you wrap the wire round in the same place each time.

L Crimping pliers
These have two notches in the jaws, one to squeeze your crimp and the other to fold it neatly over (p. 19). While flat-nose pliers can be used for crimping, it's easy to flatten the crimp too much.

M Split-ring pliers
Split rings are very fiddly to open, so if you are going to use them a lot it's worth investing in pliers with a tip designed to open them.

N Nylon jaw pliers
The softer surface of these pliers makes them suitable for straightening wire and working with aluminum wire, which is soft and easily damaged.

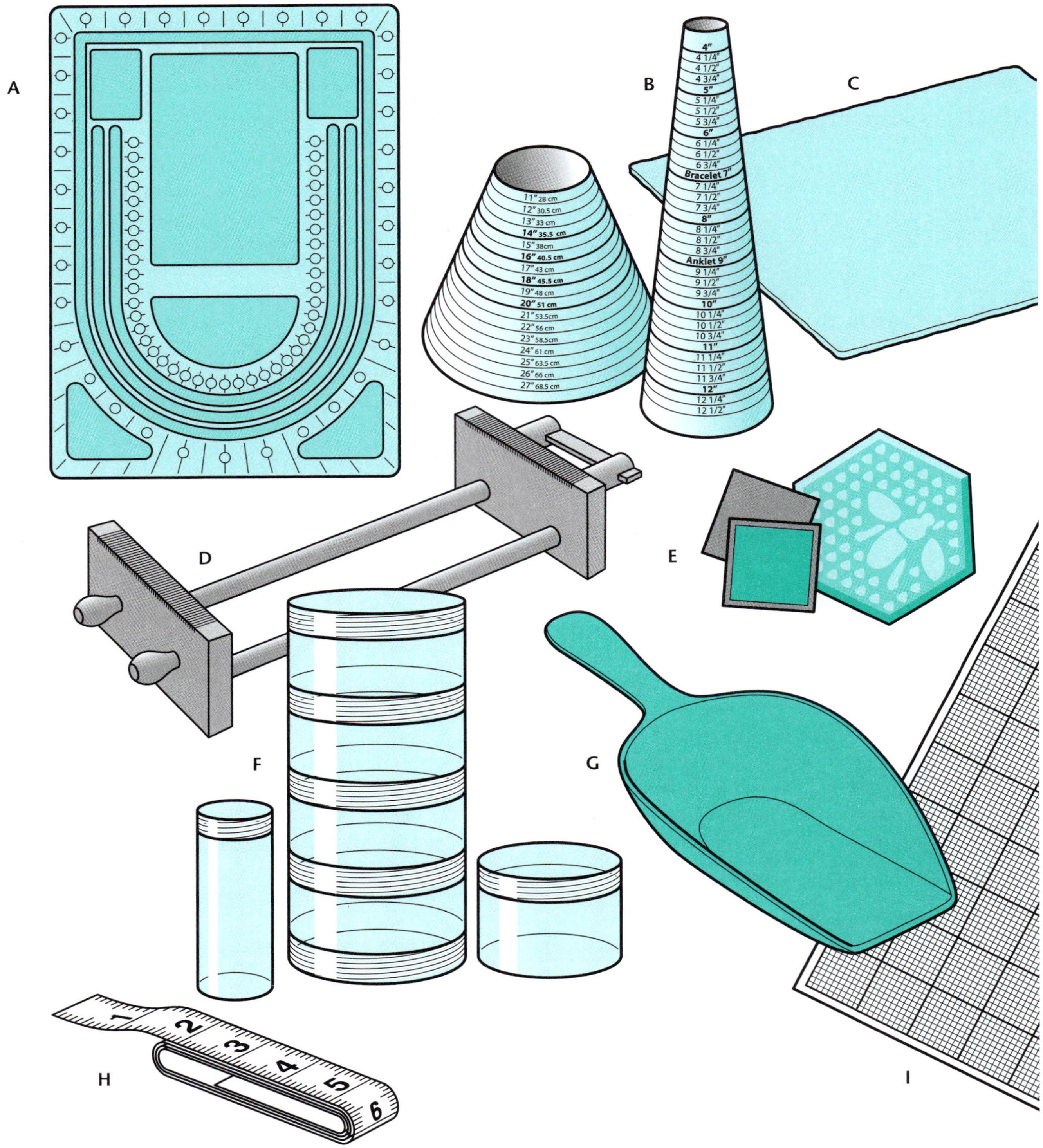
A
B
C
4"
4 1/4"
4 1/2"
4 3/4"
5"
5 1/4"
5 1/2"
5 3/4"
6"
6 1/4"
6 1/2"
6 3/4"
Bracelet 7"
7 1/4"
7 1/2"
7 3/4"
8"
8 1/4"
8 1/2"
8 3/4"
Anklet 9"
9 1/4"
9 1/2"
9 3/4"
10"
10 1/4"
10 1/2"
10 3/4"
11"
11 1/4"
11 1/2"
11 3/4"
12"
12 1/4"
12 1/2"
11" 28 cm
12" 30.5 cm
13" 33 cm
14" 35.5 cm
15" 38cm
16" 40.5 cm
17" 43 cm
18" 45.5 cm
19" 48 cm
20" 51 cm
21" 53.5cm
22" 56 cm
23" 58.5cm
24" 61 cm
25" 63.5 cm
26" 66 cm
27" 68.5 cm
D
E
F
G
H
1
2
3
4
5
6
I

EQUIPMENT

As with tools, acquiring the proper equipment will help you to progress more quickly with your bead jewelry – but if your budget is limited, just buy what you strictly need as you go along and think creatively about how you can extemporize.

A Bead design board
By using one of these you can plan out your designs very carefully, placing the beads in the grooves both to see how they work aesthetically and to measure the exact length of your arrangement.

B EZ Sizer
Another useful design aid is the EZ sizer, available for both necklaces and bracelets. If you are making a piece for someone you know, you can take the measurement of their neck or wrist and check as you go along that you are getting the fit just right.

C Bead mat
By their very nature, beads are prone to roll on a hard, smooth surface and if you lay a piece of ordinary fabric on your table to create texture you will probably find your needle hooking into it as you pick up your beads. Bead mat fabric is very inexpensive and well worth buying.

D Bead loom
Looms are available in wood, plastic or metal and in a range of sizes and designs. If you are handy at DIY, or have an obliging partner or friend who is, a bead loom is very simple to make; just a frame with nails or the upright teeth of a metal comb round which to wrap the warp threads at each end will allow you to get started. A winding mechanism is more tricky to make, but if your frame is quite long you can create a lot of pieces without needing to wind the work round rollers (p. 36). However, if you find you really enjoy beadweaving, a handsome and sturdy wooden loom will add to your pleasure.

E Thread conditioner
The purpose of thread conditioner is to make the thread stronger, smoother and less likely to tangle. It is inexpensive to buy and well worth having.

F Containers
It's important to take care that your beads are stored in separate containers, since if they become mixed up you will waste a lot of time trying to sort them out again – especially if you're using seed beads. Some are sold in bags, others in containers, and the latter may or may not be suitable for longterm use. It's not difficult to source small plastic containers, ideally with screwtops so that the jar can be held steady while you take the top off; try to find clear ones so that you can see at the glance the color of the beads inside. Also add a label giving details of color, size, type, and where they are available to save time when you need to buy some more.

G Scoop
A scoop will help you to transfer your beads easily.

H Measuring tape
You will need a measuring tape for measuring necklaces, bracelets, the spaces between fringing, and so on.

I Graph paper
Mapping out your designs on graph paper allows you to create a finished diagram to follow when you are weaving beads.

BEADS

Beading is now a popular craft and the variety of beads available is correspondingly wide. While it's possible to buy extensively online, if there's a well-stocked bead store near you it's best to go in person to make your selections so that you can see the true colors and surface quality of the beads. You'll probably also find that it stimulates ideas for jewelry in a way that scrolling down a web page of cataloged items never will.

Glass beads probably offer the widest choice of color and shape, but you'll also find other materials including plastic, wood, resin, shell, bone, metal, and ceramic – and then of course there are semiprecious stones too. Ultimately, what you buy is a matter of personal taste; unless you are responding to a specific request for a piece of jewelry, you should always choose beads you will love working with.

SEED BEADS
These are the small beads used for weaving, though they have many other purposes too, from delicate necklaces and earrings to acting as decorative spacers between larger beads. They vary in size – which is, confusingly, graded differently according to their country of origin – and may be sold in strings, packets or tubes and other plastic containers. You'll find them in a range of qualities and finishes, including opaque, transparent, gloss, matt, luster, iridescent, and metallic, making them suitable for any style of jewelry, from evening wear to folk art.

BUGLES
While the choice is not as wide, these are similar to seed beads in quality and size except that they are tubular, in various lengths. This makes them ideal for combining with seed beads in fringing on a choker or in drop earrings, for example.

CUBE BEADS
Another variation in small beads is the cube shape, which provides straight edges in a design rather than the softer, rounded shapes of standard seed beads. You will also find triangular beads on sale, along with other geometric shapes such as hexagons.

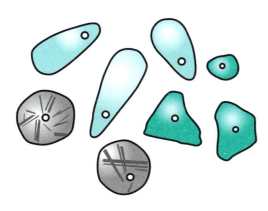

SEMIPRECIOUS BEADS

Among semiprecious stones you'll find beautiful colors, from the deep blue of lapis lazuli to purple amethyst and pink-flushed rose quartz. They may be cut and polished, faceted as for costume jewelry, or left relatively natural. The latter are the least expensive, but can be just as beautiful as the more refined version – or even more so, depending on your taste.

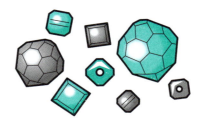

CRYSTALS

The wide range of price attached to these faceted beads is explained by the material used, which may be the finest cut glass, cheap glass or even plastic. Crystal beads come in a wide variety of colors and shapes and here paying for the best definitely brings you the most attractive beads.

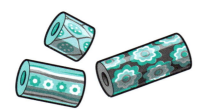

VENETIAN MILLEFIORI

Millefiori means "thousand flowers", which describes the heavily patterned nature of these beads. They have been produced by the glass workshops of Venice and Murano for hundreds of years and are made by adding individual layers of colors and shapes to molten glass, drawing it out into a rod then cutting it into slices. Thanks to the internet you can now buy them direct from Venice if you wish to, giving you a greater selection than you will find in a local bead store and adding to the pleasure of acquiring beads with such a long history.

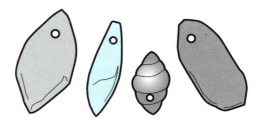

SHELL AND BONE

Natural materials such as these go well with leather thongs and other chunky threads. They would have been among the first decorative materials worn by early humans, and today they still look good treated simply with little more than a polish to give some shine and a hole drilled through to take the thread. Other natural materials given similar treatment include nuts and amber.

METAL

This term covers everything from inexpensive tin to pure gold, so the choice of design and price is enormous. Materials such as copper, brass, aluminum and various alloys are often heavily molded and patterned, giving interesting texture; you will also find beads plated with gold and silver, as well as more valuable ones made from sterling silver.

CERAMIC

Ceramic beads are sourced from all over the world and you will be able to find almost any pattern and color you could wish for. Many are still handmade, giving them a pleasing individuality. Similar in style are beads made from other materials such as papiermâché and resin. These beads are ideal for bold, flamboyant designs.

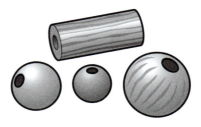

WOOD

Wooden beads are also suited to informal, folk styles of jewelry. They come in various woods, often with attractive graining and natural coloring, and in different sizes and shapes. They may also be painted and varnished; if you are so inclined, you can paint your own designs on them instead.

PART TWO:
TECHNIQUES

The techniques you will use when working with beads are generally simple and straightforward, requiring nothing more than some manual dexterity and patience. Some can only be practiced by making a piece of jewelry, but for basic techniques such as attaching fastenings it's a good idea to have a go first with just lengths of thread and the findings until you feel confident you can do what you need to neatly and efficiently.

OPENING AND CLOSING JUMP RINGS

This is something you will need to do often, and although you can easily see what you're trying to achieve there's a right way and a wrong way of going about it.

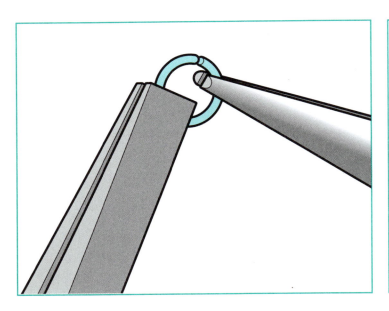

1 Take hold of your jump ring using two pairs of pliers with flat jaws, one each side of the join in the ring. Rather than holding it with the tips of the pliers, angle them sideways so that they cover more of the ring – this will make it easier for you to handle the jump ring.

2 Carefully move one pair of pliers away from you and the other towards you until you have made a gap as wide as you need. Never pull the pliers outwards and away from each other because you won't be able to restore the round shape of the jump ring.

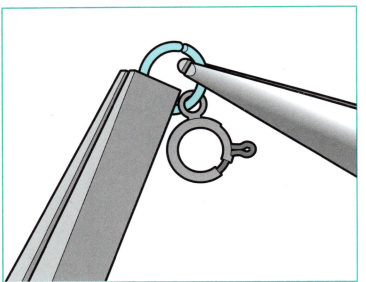

3 Once you have put the loop of the finding or chain you are using inside the jump ring, use the pliers as before and reverse the process to close the jump ring. Bring the ends a little way past each other and exert a slight inward push to make sure the gap is as small as possible.

CRIMPING

Technique with crimping pliers

Crimps have many uses, among them providing the means to attach a clasp to a length of flexible beading wire. This is done by making a loop in the wire and securing it with a crimp, using crimping pliers or flat-nose pliers. Crimps come in different sizes and you will need to use the right size for your wire and your crimping pliers too. If in doubt, check with your supplier or visit the web sites of the wire manufacturers, where you will find details of the crimp sizes needed.

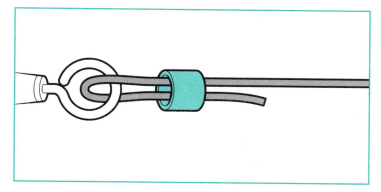

1 Pass the beading wire through the crimp, through the clasp you are using, then back through the crimp again to form a loop.

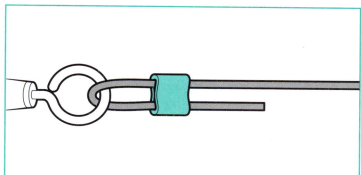

2 Making sure that the two pieces of wire are side by side rather than crossing each other, place the crimp in the notch nearest to the handle of your pliers. Squeeze carefully to flatten the crimp and pull gently on the wires to check they are tightly held.

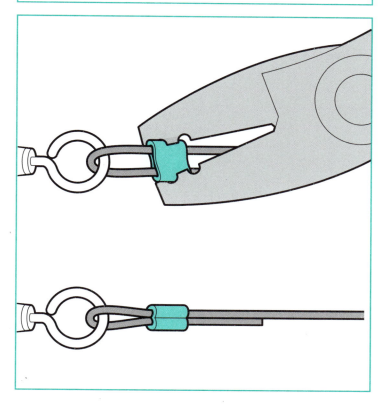

3 Next, transfer the crimp to the notch nearest the end of the plier jaws, turning it so that this time one wire is above the other. Squeeze the crimp with the pliers to fold it over and give it a rounded shape.

Technique with flat-nose pliers

Thread the wire through the crimp and clasp as before then squeeze the crimp with the pliers. Check that the wire is securely held. These pliers produce a flattened crimp with square corners – check to make sure that they aren't sharp, and if necessary smooth them with a file.

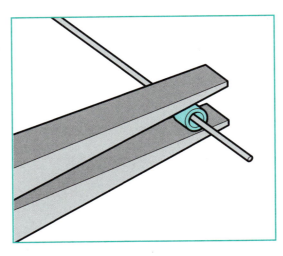 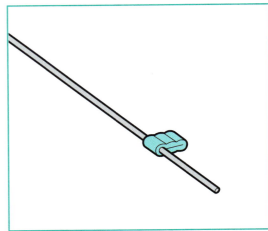

Using crimps on cord and leather

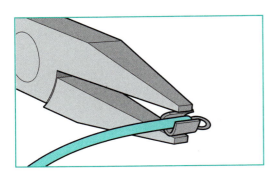 

1 Cut a straight end on your length of cord or leather and lay it in the crimp. With your flat-nose pliers, fold one end of the crimp securely over, then repeat with the other side.

2 With a crimp at each end of your cord or leather thong, it's then easy to attach a fastener.

Fabric cord

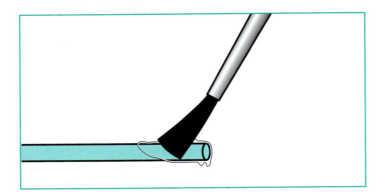 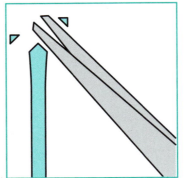 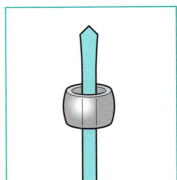

1 To stiffen fabric cord so that you can easily thread the beads onto it, cover the end with craft glue or clear nail polish to a length of about 1½ in [4 cm]. This can be done either by painting it on or simply dipping the cord into the container.

2 If the holes in the beads are quite small in relation to the cord, you'll find it helpful to cut the end of the cord to a point once the glue or nail polish is dry. Before crimping, cut off the treated end, leaving just enough to fit into the crimp.

WORKING WITH CALOTTES

Attaching calottes

The end of flexible beading wire can be made ready for a fastener by knotting the wire and covering the knot with a calotte. Calottes have a groove cut into the side edges or a hole in the hinge or side. The steps below show you how to use one with a groove; for one with a hole in the hinge, you will need to make the knot after passing the wire through the hole, as the knot should be too big to pull back out of it.

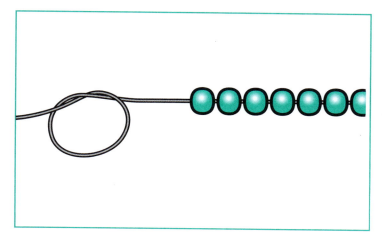

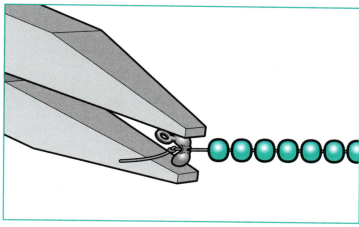

1 Once you have threaded your beads, secure one end of the wire to your work surface and tie an overhand knot (p. 28) in the other end.

2 Center your knot in the calotte then gently squeeze the calotte over the knot, using flat-nose pliers.

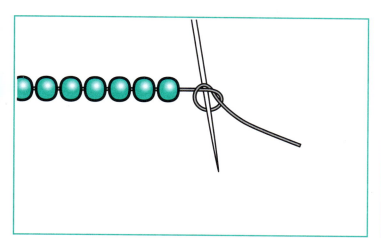

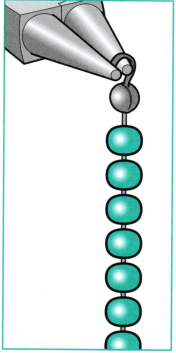

3 To attach the calotte at the other end of the wire, make another overhand knot then, using your awl or a large needle, slide the knot close to the beads. Add the calotte as before.

4 Some calottes have a closed loop to take a fastener, while others have just a length of wire. In the case of the latter, just form a loop with your round-nose pliers.

Using calottes for multiple strands

Larger calottes can also be used to finish a piece with multiple strands joined together by a knot or crimps.

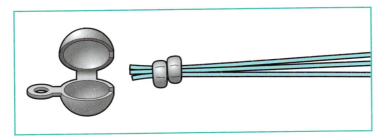

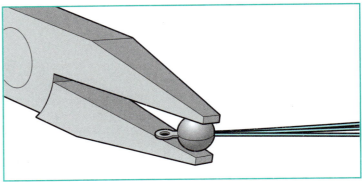

I Trim the strands to a neat ending then enclose them in the calotte.

2 Using flat-nose pliers, squeeze the calotte together tightly enough to secure the threads.

CRIMPING ONTO AN END BAR

End bars with multiple loops make an attractive way to finish a bracelet or necklace. You can make the piece first without attaching either end, but in the case of a bracelet with its shorter length you'll find it easier to put on the first end bar before you start working with your beads.

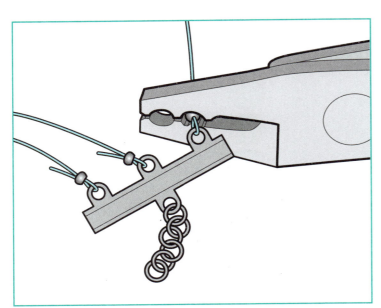

Pass each of your threads through a crimp and a loop on the end bar then back through the crimp. Finish the crimp with your crimping pliers as shown on p. 19, then trim off the end of the thread.

Once you have finished threading your design, attach the other end bar by crimping the wires as before.

ATTACHING TO AN END CONE

If you prefer your multistrand necklace, bracelet or earrings to be gathered together at the ends rather than spaced apart, using an end cone is the answer. These come in a range of styles, so take care to choose one that suits the style of the bead design you will be using.

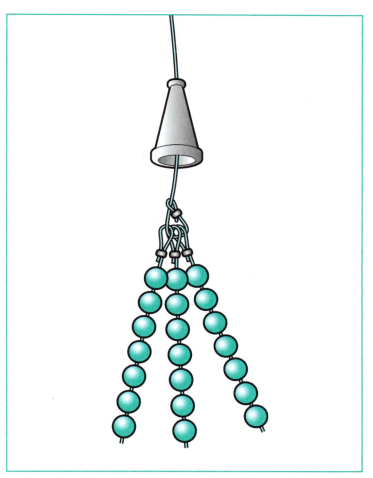

1 Make a small loop at the end of each of the wires, using crimps. Cut two lengths of beading wire and crimp a small loop at the end of each. Next, pass the uncrimped end of one of the wires through the loops at each end of your multistrand design and thread it back through its own loop.

2 Tighten the lengths of wire to bring the multistrands together. Check that they hang together attractively and then pull the wire through an end cone, hiding the gathered loops inside it.

You now need to attach a fastener to the wire, allowing a little space from the end cone to make handling the fastener easier. Decorate this short length of wire with beads that complement the design and crimp them on to the fastener.

MAKING A LOOP ON A HEADPIN OR EYEPIN

The quickest way to make a drop earring or a dangle on a necklace is to use a headpin or an eyepin – all you need to do is to turn a loop at the top once you have slid your beads on it. If the beads you are using have a hole big enough for them to pass over the stop at the bottom of the pin, add a smaller bead at the bottom of the pin to act as a larger stop.

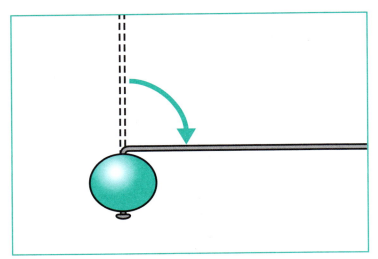

1 Thread your bead (or beads) on to the headpin or eyepin. Making sure that the bead is resting firmly on the bottom of the pin, bend the wire across the top of the bead at a right-angle, using either your fingers or your flat-nose pliers.

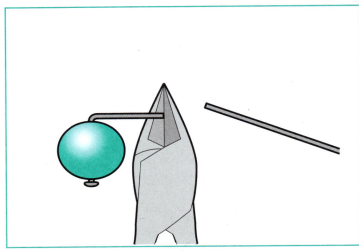

2 Using wirecutters, cut the wire to a length of about ½ in [1 cm] from the bead.

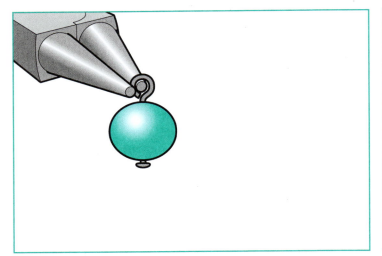

3 With the cut end facing towards you, grip the wire with round-nose pliers and roll the wire away from you to form a loop.

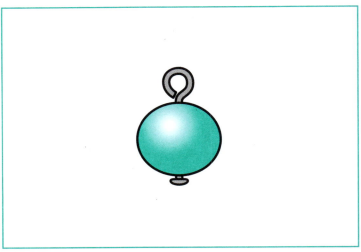

4 The finished loop will now be centered above the bead, ensuring that it will hang straight.

MAKING A WRAPPED LOOP

A wrapped loop is stronger and more secure than a simple loop and also contributes a decorative quality.

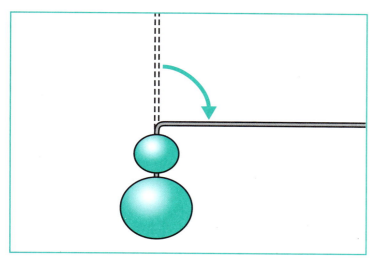

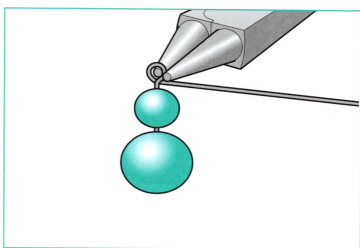

1 Cut the wire to a length of at least 1¼ in [3 cm] above the last bead then, using flat-nose pliers, bend the wire at a right-angle as for a simple loop but this time leaving a gap between the top bead and the angle.

2 With your round-nose pliers, hold the wire close to the angle and then wrap the remaining wire round one jaw of the pliers to form a loop.

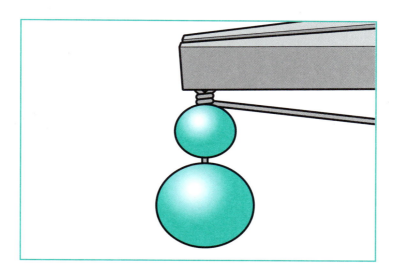

3 Take the loop in a firm grip with your flat-nose pliers and wind the tail of the wire round the stem repeatedly until it encloses the whole length from the top bead to the loop. Trim off the end.

PROJECT: MAKING A PAIR OF EARRINGS

From this project you'll discover just how quick and easy it is to make a pretty piece of jewelry. Using large beads gives the most eyecatching result in the shortest time, but you will probably have to add some smaller beads too in order to prevent the large one falling off the headpin or eyepin. They will also add a more graceful and decorative effect.

Headpins and eyepins are sold in both hard and soft quality. For earrings, use the hard version. You will also need two earring findings – fish hooks are shown here, but the procedure is the same for any style you would like to use.

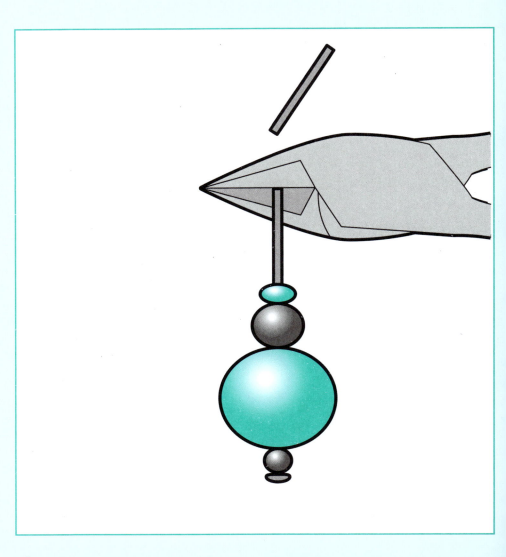

I Thread at least one small bead on to one of the headpins or eyepins, followed by your large bead and then a few smaller ones – the number and type you use is a matter of choice, both for aesthetic appeal and the desired length (of the earrings). Once all your beads are threaded, cut the wire about ½ in [1 cm] above the beads.

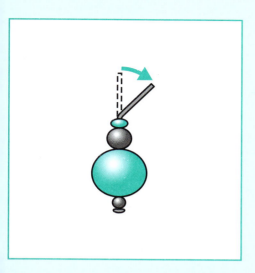

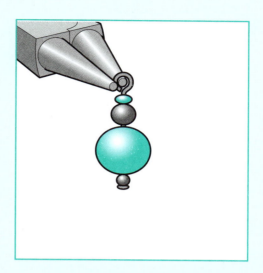

2 Holding the beads between the thumb and fingers of your left hand (if you are right-handed), grip the wire immediately above the beads with round-nose pliers and bend it towards you at a 45-degree angle.

3 Grip the end of the wire with the tips of the pliers and roll the wire away from you to form a loop – you may need to move the pliers to complete it.

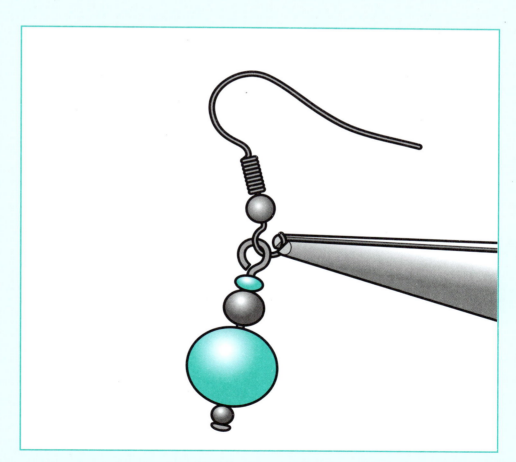

4 With your pliers, open the loop of one of the earwires by bending it a little to the side. Slip the loop of the earring into the earwire loop and close the latter up, using your pliers. Check that everything looks as it should, then make the second earring.

KNOTS

You will often need to knot threads to tie off ends and join lengths of thread. Reef (square) and overhand are the main knots used, and while they are reliable you can make doubly sure they won't come undone by putting a little glue on them.

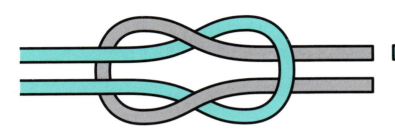

REEF KNOT

This knot is used to join two threads. With the ends of the threads facing each other, lay the left thread over and under the right and bring the end of it upwards so both ends are facing each other. Pass it over the left thread and then bring it up through the loop you have made.

OVERHAND KNOT

The overhand knot has myriad uses, from tying multiple threads together to forming knots between beads. Take the tail of the thread over to make a loop, then pass the tail over the thread and up through the loop.

Knotting to finish

If you have made a simple bead necklace that is long enough to go over the head, the only means of fastening you need is a reef knot.

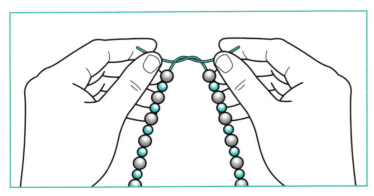

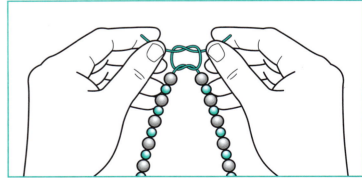

1 Measure the length that you wish the necklace to be and allow about 4 in [10 cm] extra thread at each end for the knot.

2 Make a reef knot and tighten it securely, checking before you do so that it's not so tight against the beads that it is making the necklace stiff to handle. Trim the ends of the threads and tuck them out of sight.

Knotting between beads

This is done both for decorative purposes and for security in the case of valuable stones or pearls – if the thread breaks, only one or two beads will fall off and the rest will remain safely held. Use overhand knots, which can be moved along the thread to put them into the correct position; if the holes in the beads are bigger than the knots, make a double overhand knot simply by passing the thread through a second time.

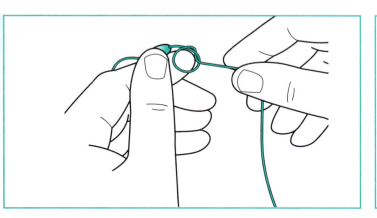

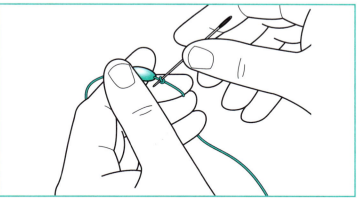

1 Cut a length of thread that is at least two and half times the length you wish your finished piece to be. Remember that if you overestimate, you have only wasted a small amount of thread; if you underestimate, all your work is wasted! Attach a fastener to the thread, then thread your first bead and make an overhand knot.

2 Put your awl or a blunt needle into the knot and slide it up against the bead. Once it is in the right position, tighten the knot as you remove the needle. Continue making a knot after adding each bead until the piece is finished.

Sliding bead fastener

A very easy way to make a fastening for a thick thread such as a leather thong is to use a bead. This may be one of the same beads you have chosen for your design, or a different one that complements them. Apart from its simplicity, this method has the advantage that you can adjust the length of the necklace by sliding the bead up or down.

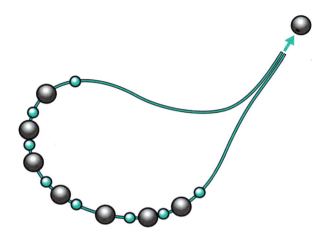

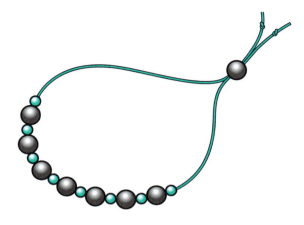

1 Cut a thong to the desired length and thread on the beads for your design. Once it is finished, slide both ends of the thong through the fastener bead.

2 Finally, make an overhand knot at each end of the thong to prevent the bead from falling off.

PROJECT: FRINGING A SCARF

Adding a fringe of beads to fabric is very easy to do, and it's a look that is effective on clothing, soft furnishing and lampshades. It also offers you a chance to turn a scarf, pashmina or shawl into a special gift that can't be bought at the mall. Choose beads of a size and color that will complement the fabric you are decorating, and also bear weight in mind; a silk scarf won't benefit from heavy beads swinging from it.

Ideally, start off with the correct length of thread so that you don't need to knot in a new one as you work along the scarf. You can arrive at a rough estimate by measuring the width of the scarf and the number and length of the fringes, remembering that each one will account for double the length of thread. However, depending on your design, this may mean a length that's hard to work with, in which case an extra discreet knot may be best.

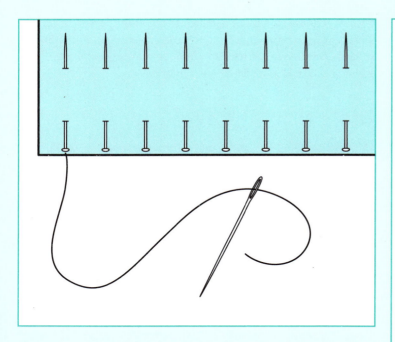

I The distance between the fringes is a matter of choice, partly depending on the type of fabric and the size of the beads, but once you've made your decision you'll need to get the spacing consistent. To do this, lay the fabric flat on your work surface and, using a ruler, mark the spacing with pins. Thread up a long beading needle and attach the thread to the fabric with a double knot where your first beads will hang.

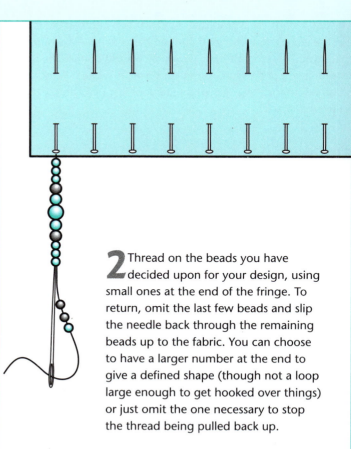

2 Thread on the beads you have decided upon for your design, using small ones at the end of the fringe. To return, omit the last few beads and slip the needle back through the remaining beads up to the fabric. You can choose to have a larger number at the end to give a defined shape (though not a loop large enough to get hooked over things) or just omit the one necessary to stop the thread being pulled back up.

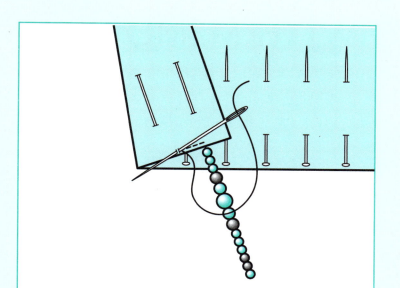

3 Take the needle along the hem of the fabric on the wrong side, using small, unobtrusive running stitches to reach the next pin. Continue until you have made all the fringes in your design and then finish off the thread securely.

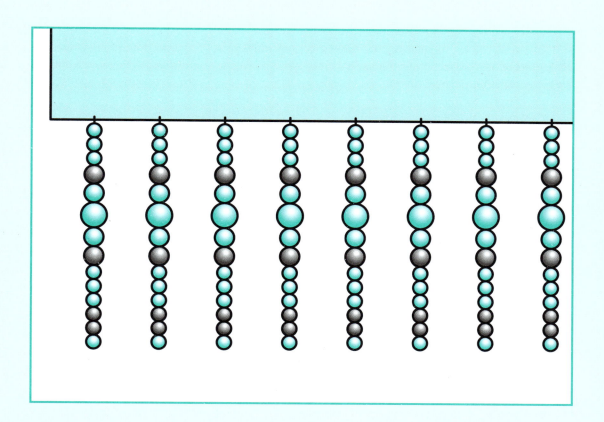

WORKING WITH MEMORY WIRE

Memory wire is precoiled and strong, making it excellent threading material for necklaces and bracelets. Because it retains its coil you can make what appear to be multistrand pieces but are in fact a continuous length.

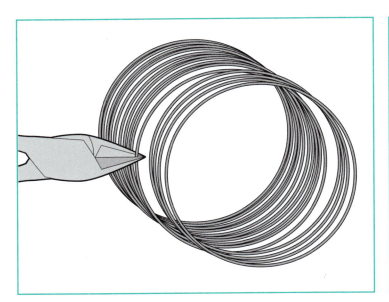

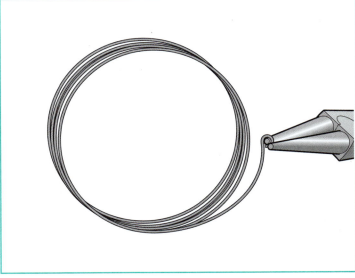

1 Cut the wire to the required length, using special memory wire cutters or heavy-duty cutters from a DIY store. Take care with the cut ends, as they can be sharp.

2 With strong round-nose pliers, roll one end of the wire into a loop. When you roll the loops at the end of the wire, always turn them outwards so that they don't rub against the wearer's neck or wrist.

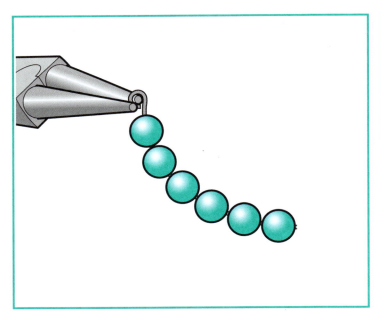

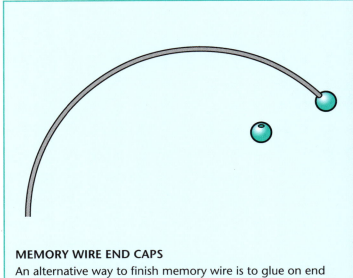

3 After threading on your beads, roll a loop at the other end of the wire.

MEMORY WIRE END CAPS
An alternative way to finish memory wire is to glue on end caps, which have a hole to take the wire and are available in colors to match the wire you are using.

MAKING A WIRE COIL

Coils made from metal wire are an attractive way of enhancing drop earrings or chains. If you plan to use them at the end of earrings you will only need to make one loop to attach them; to use them between beads and the earring findings, or as spacers in a necklace, make a loop at both top and bottom.

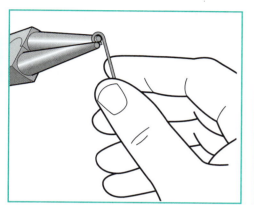

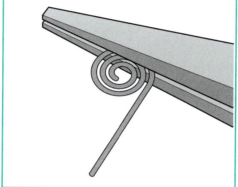

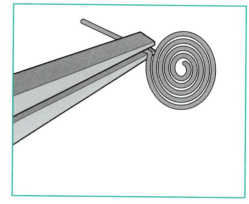

1 First, cut a length of wire and form a loop as small as you can with the tips of your round-nose pliers.

2 Hold the loop with your flat-nose pliers, taking care to grip it firmly but without damaging the wire. With your fingers, coil the wire round the central loop.

3 When the coil has reached the size you want, bend the wire away from the loop at a right angle, using the pliers.

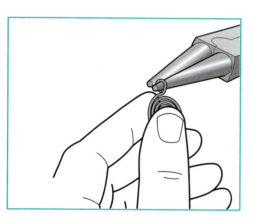

4 Cut the wire and form either a simple or wrapped loop (p. 25).

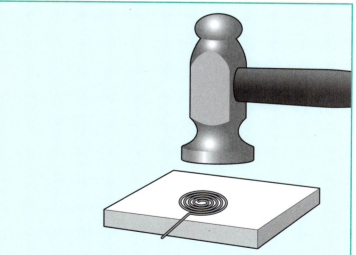

HAMMERED WIRE
Hammering a wire coil gives it extra texture and an attractive informal and even archaic look. It is best done before making the loop so that you can retain a length of wire with which you can hold the coil steady while keeping your fingers safely away from the hammer. Lay the coil on your block and use the flat end of your hammer, taking care not to tilt it as the edges will strike the coil instead, making sharp dents.

PROJECT: MAKING A SIMPLE NECKLACE

Using cord and chunky beads is a good way to achieve an impressive result in a short space of time. As a beginner, you'll find it confidence-building to have made something so attractive and wearable with such ease.

For this project you will need a length of satin cord (see Step 1), beads of your choice, two cord crimps and a clasp. You may prefer to use a different type to the one shown here; a toggle clasp would also be well suited to a bold piece of jewelry such as this.

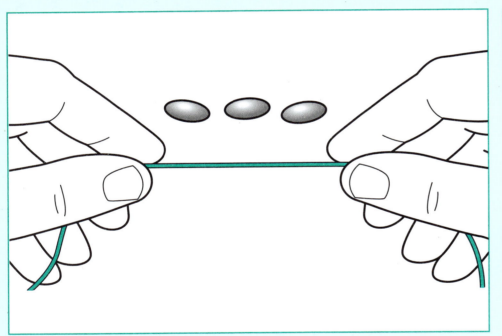

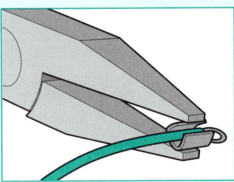

2 Crimp one end of the cord, making sure it is securely fastened (p. 20). Prepare the other end to make it easier to thread the beads (p. 20).

1 First, decide how long you want your necklace to be; you may want it to lie at the base of your throat, or perhaps you would prefer one that hangs much lower. Then work out how many beads will fit onto that length, from which you will know the number of knots to make. Allow about 1 in [2.5 cm] for each knot, plus the overall length. If in doubt, it's always best to err on the side of generosity.

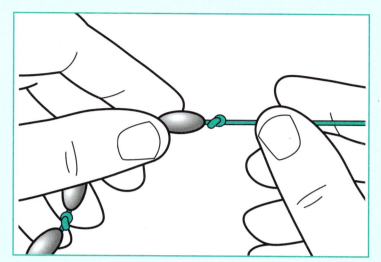

3 Make an overhand knot (p. 28) in the cord then thread your first bead. Continue alternating knots and beads until you have made a necklace of the length you require.

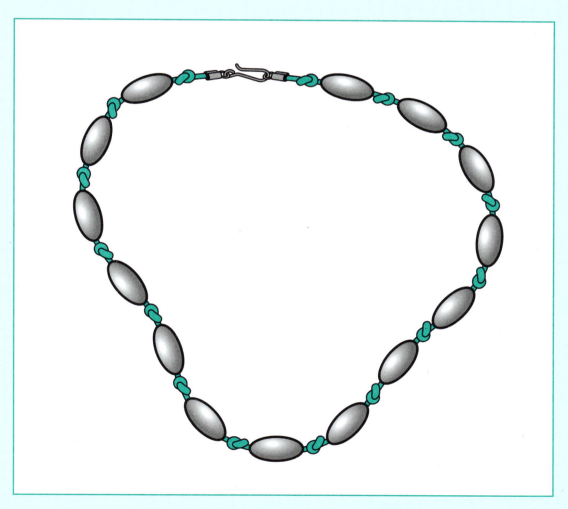

4 Finish the end of the cord with a cord crimp. Using pliers, open the loop at the end of the clasp sideways. Slip the opened loop into the loop of the clasp and then close it with the pliers.

PART THREE:
BEADWEAVING

Weaving beads on a loom gives you the ability to make intricate patterns for belts, bracelets, chokers, purses, decorations for cushions and many other uses. You may want to invent your own patterns or copy designs that you like, adapting them to fit onto graph paper with each square representing a bead; easiest of all, you can now use computer software to turn any image into a graph pattern. You will find two suggested designs on page 48.

SETTING UP A LOOM

The first step in beadweaving is to set up the warp threads on your loom. There are two methods of doing this: individual warp or single warp, also known as pulled warp or endless warp. The latter method avoids the task of finishing off a number of threads, but you'll need to take great care when working that you don't put your needle through a warp thread; to finish the work you need to pull all the threads through to leave one long thread remaining, and once you have mistakenly anchored a warp thread with a weft thread this becomes impossible to do.

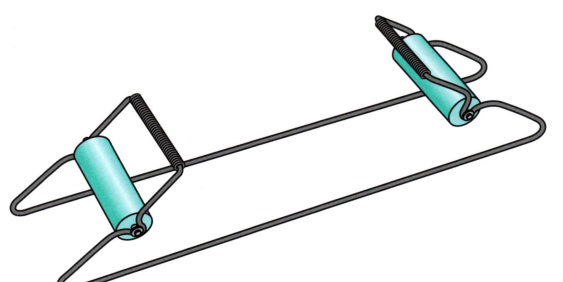

Always consider whether you need to have an odd number of beads in each row – this allows you to have a central bead in your design and also make a buttonhole (p. 47).

Individual warp

Using strong synthetic thread, first cut the warp threads to the length of your proposed piece plus at least 6 in [15 cm] at each end to attach to the loom. You'll need one more thread than the number of beads in a row, and it's a good idea to put two threads at each side – you'll have extra threads to finish off, but the beadwork will be stronger. So, if your design is seven beads across, you'll need ten threads.

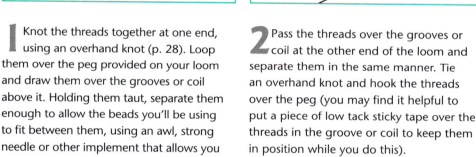

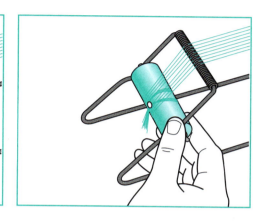

1 Knot the threads together at one end, using an overhand knot (p. 28). Loop them over the peg provided on your loom and draw them over the grooves or coil above it. Holding them taut, separate them enough to allow the beads you'll be using to fit between them, using an awl, strong needle or other implement that allows you to pick up the threads one by one.

2 Pass the threads over the grooves or coil at the other end of the loom and separate them in the same manner. Tie an overhand knot and hook the threads over the peg (you may find it helpful to put a piece of low tack sticky tape over the threads in the groove or coil to keep them in position while you do this).

3 Adjust the rollers so that there are roughly equal lengths of thread at each end, then tighten one roller. Turn the other until the threads are tautly held, then tighten it.

Single warp

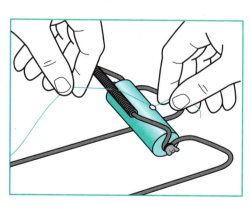

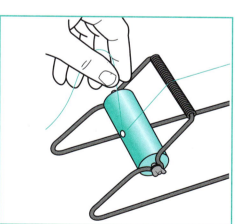

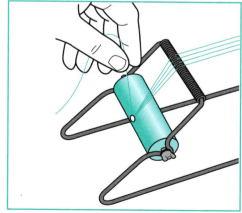

1 You'll need a considerable length of thread for this method, using it straight off the reel. Tie the thread to the peg at one end of the loom, run it through a groove and then take it down to the matching groove at the other end of the loom.

2 Loop the thread round the second peg and then, keeping it taut, take it back down to the end where you started, placing it in the grooves at the correct distance to take your beads. Continue until you have completed a warp of the width your design requires, then tie the thread to the last peg.

STARTING TO WEAVE

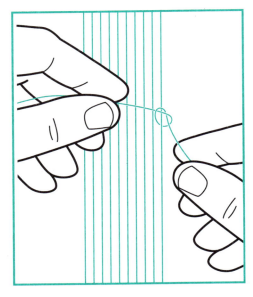

1 First, check that you will be able to pass the needle and thread you plan to use several times – your weft thread can be less sturdy than the warp thread. Thread a length onto a long, fine beading needle, using as much as you feel you can comfortably manage without tangling, so that you don't need to add new thread too often. Using an overhand knot, tie the thread onto the outside warp thread.

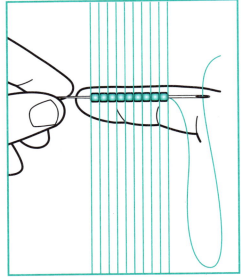

2 Following your pattern, pick up the first row of beads on your needle and push them up *under* the warp threads, one bead between each thread. Pull the needle and thread all the way through the beads, keeping your other index finger beneath them for support.

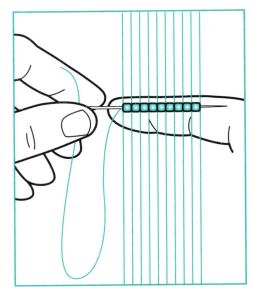

3 Bring needle and weft thread over the outer warp thread. Now pass the needle in the opposite direction, through the beads *above* the warp thread, and pull the thread through until it connects with the warp thread, forming a firm edge.

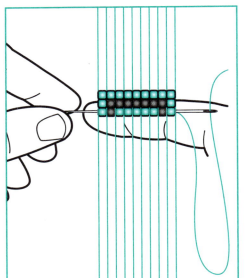

4 Repeat for the following rows, pushing each row of beads snugly up against the previous one as you go.

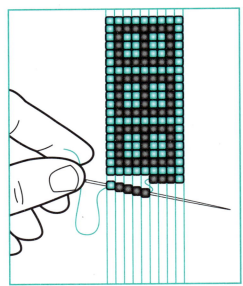

5 If you run out of thread, knot in a new length between two beads within the row, as the join is less obtrusive than at the edges. Sew in the tails once you have taken the beading off the loom.

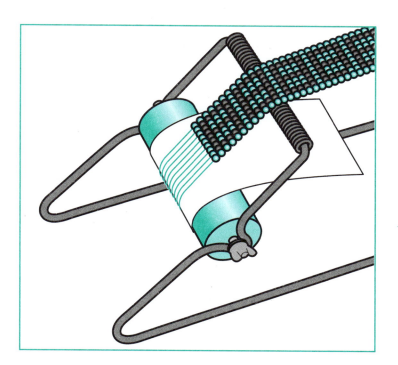

6 If the piece you are making is to be longer than the distance between the grooves that space the warp, loosen the rollers and wind the piece along as far as is necessary. If this means that the beadwork will lie over the peg, provide a little padding in the form of a piece of card.

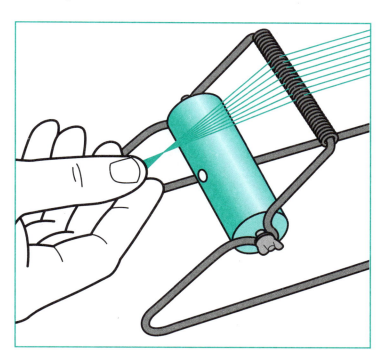

7 To take your work off the loom, simply loosen the rollers and lift the threads clear of the pegs.

INCREASING AND DECREASING

Increasing

Providing variation in the width of your woven piece can be done by simply adding or subtracting the number of beads in a row. If you will be increasing, don't forget to allow for that when you set up your warp threads.

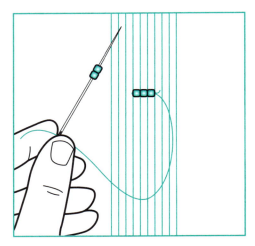

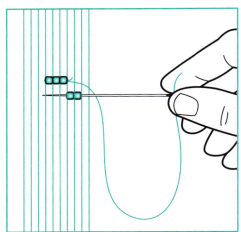

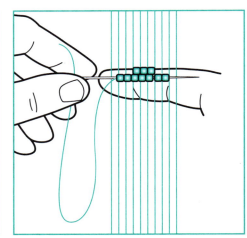

1 At the end of a row, bring the weft thread out above the beads and pick up the number of extra beads you want to increase by.

2 Lay them on top of the warp as an extension to the new row to come, push them down and pass the needle through them beneath the warp threads.

3 Pick up the remaining beads, including any to form a matching increase at the other edge, push them up through the warp and pass the needle back through above the warp, including the beads you first added.

Decreasing

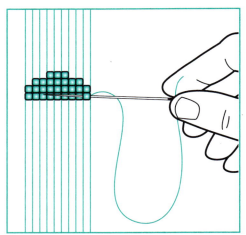

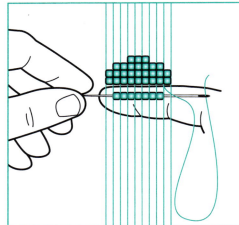

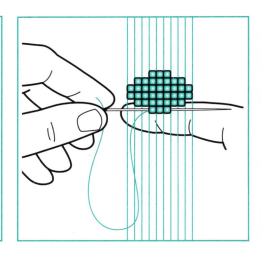

1 After completing the last full-width row, take the needle over the outer warp thread and put it back through the number of beads on that row by which you want to decrease. Bring the needle out at the top then pass it over the new outer thread of the warp to the underside.

2 Pick up the smaller number of beads for the shorter row and weave into place in the usual way.

3 Continue to decrease until the woven beads have reached the shape you want to make.

MAKING AN INTEGRATED FRINGE

While you can add a fringe after your woven panel is finished, it is often easier to do it as you go. If you plan it out on your graph paper along with the rest of the design, you will know exactly the point at which to start adding the fringe.

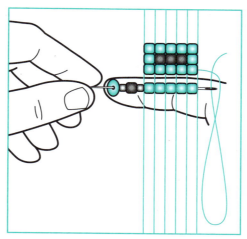

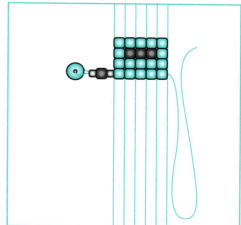

1 When you reach the row of beads where the fringe starts, pick up the additional beads, remembering you will need at least one to pass the thread back round.

2 Supporting the extra beads with your finger, pass the needle round the end bead and then back along the other beads in the fringe and the row on the warp threads.

3 A choker looks good with a graduated shape; just plan your design so that the fringing lengthens and then shortens again once you are past the central point of the choker.

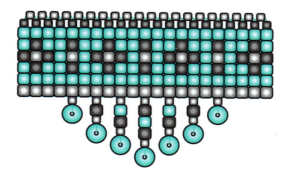

MAKING LOOPED EDGINGS

Loops cannot be integrated and must be added afterwards. However, for stability, you need to thread through the beads on the warp as before.

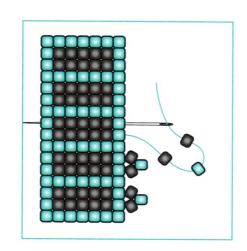

1 Knot in a thread at the top of the row beneath which you want the loop to hang. Pass the needle through the beads on the warp, then pick up the beads for the loop. Thread the needle back up the row where you want the loop to terminate.

2 Continue to add further loops to the design you have chosen; graduated lengths and overlapping loops work well.

FINISHING OFF

When using the individual warp method, you will have numerous tails of thread to deal with to make a neat finish. There are several ways to do this, either disguising them or making a feature of them.

Sewing in

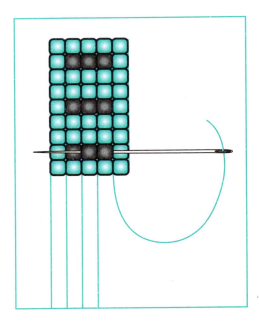

Thread each tail onto a beading needle and pass it through a few beads. Make a knot by taking the needle behind a warp thread in the weaving to make a loop. Pass the needle through the loop and tighten, then thread the needle through a few more beads before trimming off the thread as close to the beadwork as you can. Any tails on the side edges, where you have joined in new thread, can be treated in the same way.

Weaving in

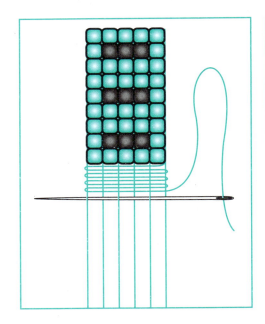

1 Before removing the beadwork from the loom, weave the weft thread in and out of the warp threads to make a panel about ¼ in [8 mm] wide.

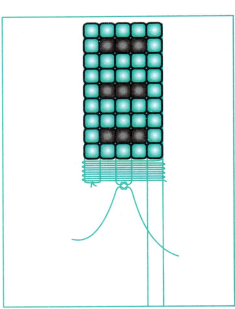

2 Lift the beadwork off the loom then tie the warp threads together in pairs. Trim them close to the knots. You can then attach a fastener to the neatly woven panel or, if you are using a backing for your beadwork, fold it beneath the beadwork and cover it with the backing.

Braiding

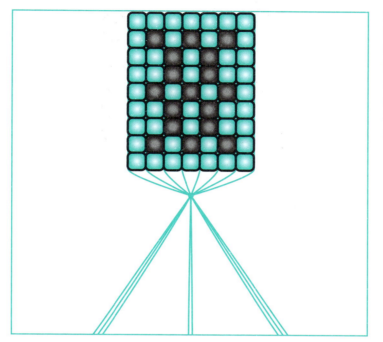

Separate your warp threads into three bundles and braid them neatly, finishing with a knot. It doesn't matter if the number of threads isn't exactly divisible by three as they aren't thick enough for the disparity to be evident.

Weaving to the center

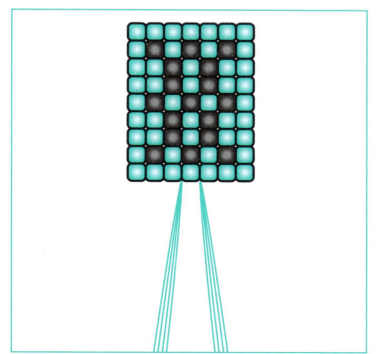

Weave your warp threads through the beads at the end of the piece so that they all exit from the center. Knot them together and enclose them in a calotte, to which you can then attach a fastener.

FASTENINGS

While the commercial fastenings used for all types of necklaces, chokers and bracelets can be attached to woven bead panels, making a fastening that incorporates beads is a particularly attractive touch.

Loop and toggle

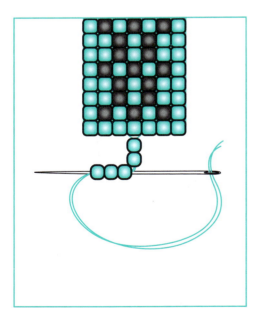

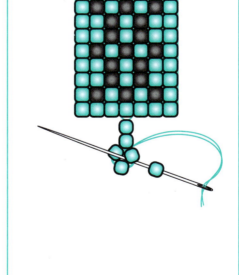

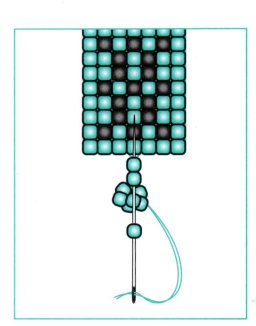

1 When you sew in the warp threads after finishing your weaving (p. 42), leave two threads in the center of your woven panel. Thread these onto a beading needle and slip five seed beads onto the thread. Pass the needle back through the last three beads and pull them into a circle.

2 Pick up a single bead with your needle and pass the needle through the circle. Build up a toggle by adding more beads, one at a time, in the same way.

3 To finish, take the threads back through the first two beads that form a stem to the toggle, pass them through a few beads in the woven panel, then knot and trim them.

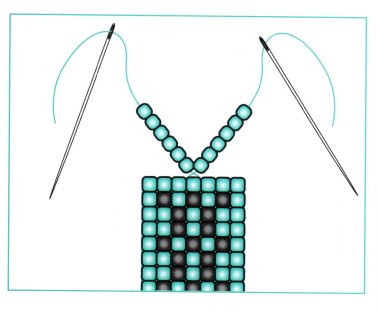

4 At the other end, sew in the warp threads leaving two in the center as before. Thread them on to two needles and pick up half the beads intended for the loop with each needle – you need a loop big enough to go over the toggle without much difficulty, but not so large that the toggle will slip out.

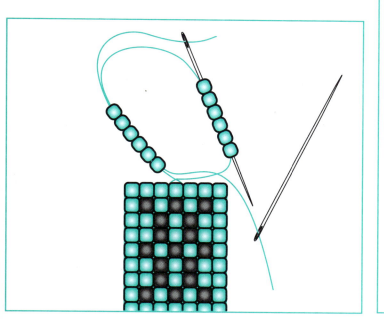

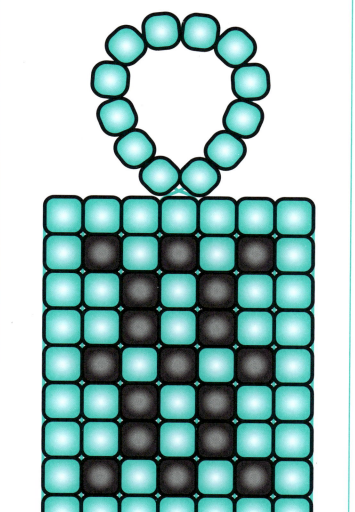

5 Pass each needle through the beads on the opposite thread so that they are all on a double thread; if you wish, pass one needle back through the whole loop to make a stronger three-thread loop. Finish off the tails as in Step 3.

Loop and button

As a variation on a loop and toggle fastening, use a pretty button instead, attached to the woven panel by a short length of single beads; thread a central warp thread on to the needle then pass it through the beads, through the hole in the button and then back down through the beads again.

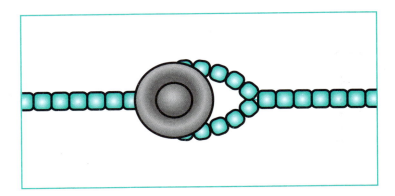

Loop and decorated bead

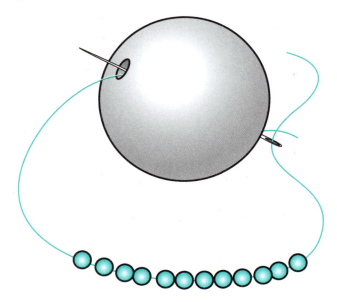

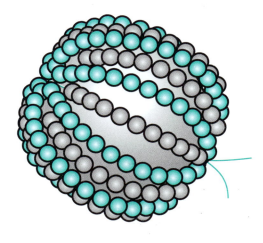

1 Anchor the tail of a long thread then pass it through the hole in a large bead. Pick up enough seed beads to fill the thread as far as the other end of the hole, then pass the needle back round and pick up more beads.

2 Continue until the big bead is largely covered with seed beads, then tie the ends of the thread together. If you wish to have a really solid effect, you can also pick up beads in small numbers at a time and take them round the circumference of the bead, passing the needle through the first set of beads as you go. Make a loop at the other end of the woven panel as before.

Bead and buttonhole

To make a buttonhole in your woven panel, you will need to have an odd number of beads. The slot can only be narrow, so check carefully that you are making it long enough for your bead to pass through it.

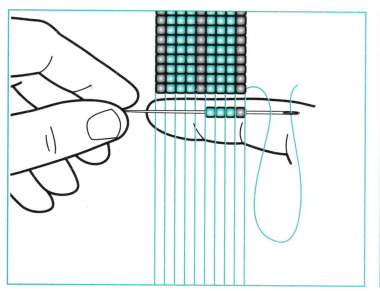

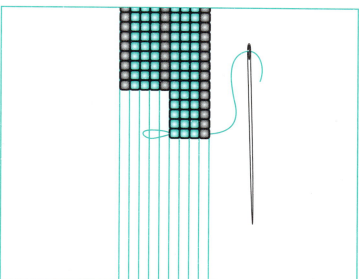

1 Pick up half the normal number of beads (minus the central bead) needed for the row and push them up through the warp threads. Pass the needle through above the warp, then take the needle back again below the warp.

2 Continue to add short rows until you have the necessary length. Weave the thread back through the rows, pulling the needle out at the end of the last full row.

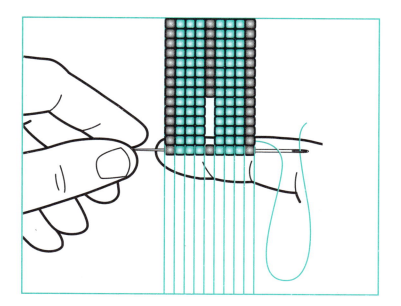

3 Once you have made a matching number of short rows on the other side, bead across the whole width for about three rows to finish making the buttonhole and the woven panel itself.

BEADWEAVING DESIGNS

The designs shown here are examples of two very different visual styles, the first sinuous and floral and the second geometric, in the style of Native American and African beadwork. For the first, you could use any type of seed bead, from opaque and bright to translucent and in more subtle colors for a more Victorian feel; for the second, brightly colored opaque beads are best, partly to stay faithful to the origins of this style and also because they better show the strong geometry of the patterning.

These designs are easy to follow, should you wish to make them; otherwise, just study them as an example of how to work out a pattern of color and shape on graph paper for your own designs.

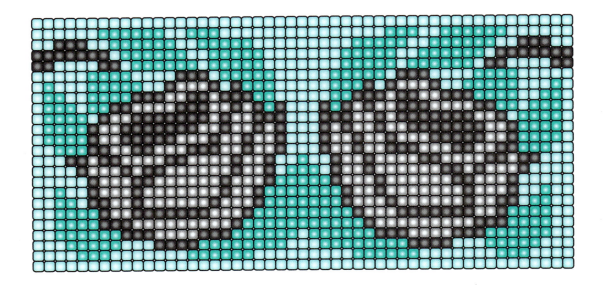

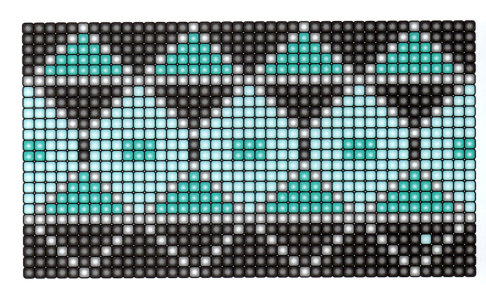